DENNIS FIRE ENGINES

BARRY HUTCHINSON

AMBERLEY

First published 2015

Amberley Publishing
The Hill, Stroud
Gloucestershire, GL5 4EP

www.amberley-books.com

British Library Cataloguing in Publication Data.
A catalogue record for this book is available from the British Library.

ISBN 978 1 4456 4607 7 (print)
ISBN 978 1 4456 4608 4 (ebook)

Typeset in 10pt on 13pt Sabon.
Typesetting and Origination by Amberley Publishing.
Printed in the UK.

Contents

Introduction

For over a hundred years if you heard the clang of a fire engine bell or the wail of a fire engine siren coming down a street in Britain, the name on the front of the engine making the noise would most likely be DENNIS.

John and Raymond Dennis started their business making bicycles in Guildford in 1895. They soon progressed to making tricycles, quadricycles and small cars using the French-made De-Dion engine. The market for the newfangled car was limited, so in 1904 they moved into commercial vehicle manufacture. From that time onwards Dennis have been synonymous with advanced vehicle design, and this can still be seen today with their hybrid bus designs.

The first Dennis fire engine was produced in 1908 and production continued for the next ninety-nine years, ending in 2007. The success of the Dennis fire engine was due to the fact that they were purpose-built as fire engines from the ground up, rather than the conversion of an existing commercial vehicle chassis. A body shop was also part of the Dennis factory at Woodbridge Hill, so it was possible for chief fire officers to purchase complete and fully integrated appliances to the highest possible standards. In 1991 the body shop, which was run by John Dennis (the grandson of the founder), was closed when the original factory moved to a modern industrial facility on the Slyfield Industrial Estate. However, the body shop re-emerged next door to the new Dennis factory as John Dennis Coach Builders, which continued the reputation for high-quality design and workmanship.

Throughout the whole history of Dennis fire engines, innovation has been the main factor in their success. It started with the novel worm-and-wheel rear differential, which was patented in 1903 and became one of the key selling features, as early conventional differentials were unreliable and prone to failure. The adoption of the turbine fire-fighting water pump compared to the conventional piston pump, which had been previously used on all steam-powered fire pumps, was an adventurous decision at the time but proved to be the correct choice. Originally using a Gwynne turbine pump, by 1922 Dennis had their own turbine pump extensively protected by patents. A similar pattern was shown by the choice of motive power. Aster Engines were originally used in their commercial vehicle chassis, but by the time of the first fire engine these had been exchanged for engines made by the Coventry-based company of White & Poppe. In 1919, Dennis purchased their engine supplier for £204,000 (£80 million today), which provided a range of technically advanced engines for their exclusive use. Even towards the end of the twentieth century, when the design of commercial vehicles had very much stabilised, Dennis broke new ground with the Dennis Rapier fire engine. Acknowledged to be the finest-handling fire engine ever produced anywhere in the world, this machine had a space-frame chassis (following Formula 1 racing car design) rather than the conventional ladder-type chassis. Many are still in use twenty years later and are reluctantly given up by fire brigade crews when replacement is mandated.

Dennis fire engines are not uniquely a sight of British roads – they were exported to all parts of the world, especially to the former British colonies.

2007 saw the last Dennis fire engine to roll off the production line. Their cabs were made by a former Dennis subsidiary that was producing large volumes of refuse vehicle cabs for Dennis Eagle, another former subsidiary of the factory at Guildford. Relatively low volumes of fire engine cabs could not now be accommodated, and, despite looking for alternative suppliers both in the UK and overseas, none could be found. However, the Dennis fire engine will survive in the hands of hundreds of enthusiasts who, during the summer rallying season, demonstrate their capability to an enthralled audience.

Dr B. A. Hutchinson,
July 2015

Peter McCombie, one of the many Dennis enthusiasts, standing by his Light Four at the Preston Hall Fire Engine Rally in 2015. After accepting the award for best pre-war appliance, he is about to set off on a 300-mile journey home with fellow enthusiast Dennis Scott in his Dennis F26.

Chapter 1

1908–1920

The first Dennis fire engine designated the N Type was supplied to Bradford Fire Brigade in 1908. A year later, the neighbouring town of Leeds took delivery of the twelfth fire engine produced by Dennis. Although equipped with the Gwynne turbine pump, mechanical piston primers had yet to be fitted. The pump was therefore primed from a central water tank mounted above the hose locker box. Later fire engines equipped with a priming pump could be identified by a full-depth rear locker, as is shown by the 1913 N Type supplied to the John Dickinson Paper Mill. Colour photography was yet to be established, however Dennis produced magnificent coloured catalogues illustrating their fire engines with particular emphasis on their overseas sales.

In 1923, the Apsley Mills Fire Brigade stand proudly in front of their machine after winning the British fire services works fire brigade competition. The appliance is very much unchanged from its delivery condition, complete with the side-mounted 'DENNIS PATENT TURBINE FIRE ENGINE' brass badges and the 'KT' air cushion tyres. This type of tyre vied with the solid rubber tyres during the early days of commercial vehicle manufacture. Individual top-hat-shaped rubber cushions were inserted through a perforated steel band. The air trapped under the cushions provided a ride quality similar to pneumatic tyres, which had yet to appear on heavy vehicles. By 1925, the rear tyres had been replaced by solid rubber tyres with a deep tread pattern. These tyres still exist on the machine today.

Sometime during the 1930s, the front wooden wheels and Dennis axle were replaced by a Bedford axle and wheels while in the ownership of the Tonbridge Rural District Council before it was passed on to the works fire brigade of Arnolds, who were fire engine bodybuilders converting mainly Land Rover-based vehicles. In preservation, the front wheels were converted back to solid rubber tyres on Dennis-cast wheels. As is common with all N Types, there are no brakes fitted to the front wheels. Primary braking is achieved by using the handbrake lever, which is outboard of the gear change lever. A pedal-operated transmission brake provides additional stopping power in emergencies. Neither brake has friction material but feature cast-iron drums with steel brake shoes.

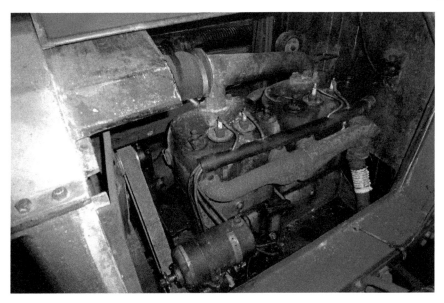

All Dennis N Types used White & Poppe engines of differing sizes. AR5232 is unusual in that it uses the relatively small 90 x 130 mm (bore and stroke) engine. This engine does not have a water pump to circulate the engine cooling water but relies on a process called thermo-syphon, where the cooler water migrates to the lower section of the radiator, creating a water flow through the engine. For this to be effective, an oversize header tank is fitted to AR5232. The engine is coupled through a power takeoff to the Gwynne fire-fighting water pump, which has a capacity of 250 gallons a minute. A design feature which Dennis introduced was the pull handle located below the centre of the pump. This opened up the pump drain valves, which was an essential task to do in winter to prevent the pump casing from cracking if the temperature fell below freezing.

By 1914, the component parts of a N Type had stabilised. Wooden spoked wheels were still in use but fitted with the more conventional solid rubber tyre. Electric lighting was starting to emerge and this machine, which was supplied new to the Greenhall Whitley brewery, had two small headlights fitted to either side of the scuttle and one small diver's helmet-style rear lamp. The electric lighting was powered by lead acid accumulators in a total loss scheme without a dynamo. The scuttle is of basic shape with a simple curve on the top edge and straight-cut edges on the other three sides. The radiator is built up from brass sheet and although it is magnificent to the eye, the soft soldered seams had a tendency to leak. In future years a cast brass and aluminium radiator would be offered as an alternative.

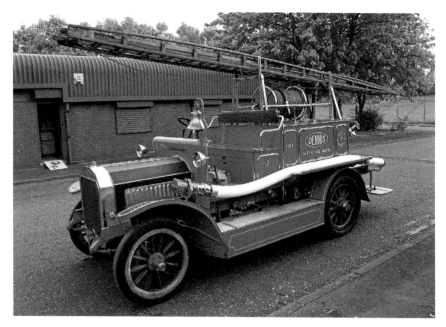

The larger Gwynne pump is now in use. With sufficient power input this is capable of delivering 1,000 gallons per minute. A hose reel is now fitted on top of the hose locker box. This is fed from the main pump. The concept of the fire engine carrying water in a body-mounted tank had still to evolve. Water pickup could only be achieved through the suction hose from a source of open of water. ED810 features over 35 feet of suction hose already coupled together for fast deployment. A perforated brass strainer is fitted to the pick-up end to prevent gravel, weed and often fish from being consumed by the pump. Turbine pumps are far more tolerant of debris entering the pump compared with piston pumps. This was one of the main selling points of the 'THE DENNIS PATENT TURBINE FIRE ENGINE'.

The engine inside of ED810 is the 45 hp variant with four separate cylinders. This is a side-valve engine with a 'T' configuration cylinder head. The exhaust valves are on the nearside, with the inlet valves on the opposite side. There are no separate cylinder heads – these are integral with the cylinder blocks. The valve springs are exposed and operated by short push rods actuated by cam shafts either side of the engine. The engine may be readied for starting by pouring petrol directly into the cylinders through the priming taps located over the exhaust valves. Located over the inlet valves are the twin spark plugs. One set is connected through a distributor to the trembler coil, and the second set is connected to the magneto. Dual ignition enhanced the reliability of this early Dennis fire engine, which was replacing a horse-drawn fire pump. However, the simplicity of a bag of oats and an apple to motivate an equine still held a great attraction for some station officers.

Electric starting was still a dream, but the dangers of hand cranking using the starting handle were well known. Kickback through the starting handle had broken many bones in hands and arms during the early years. This occurs when the engine fires as the piston is still rising, throwing the engine into the opposite direction of rotation with respect to the starting handle. The trembler coil system eliminated this risk. First the engine was turned over four times, drawing mixture into the cylinders with the ignition turned off. The trembler coil was then switched on, which provided a continuous stream of sparks. Hopefully the cylinder on the compression stroke would ignite, which would provide the motion impetus to spring the rest of the cylinders into life. The trembler coil is housed in the wooden box on the scuttle and makes a characteristic buzzing sound when operating. Once in motion, the magneto ignition can be switched on and the trembler coil turned off. Separate brass switches are used for this purpose.

By the end of 1914 Dennis had started to use the new White & Poppe engine with the cylinders cast in pairs. Two engine sizes were available. The N Type, which was supplied new to the Helensburgh Fire Brigade in 1920, had the smaller size with a bore and stroke of 115 x 150 mm, resulting in an engine capacity of 6.2 litres. Eighty years later, when SN 1549 emerged to be sold at auction, very little had changed. The bonnet still retained the original unpainted blue finish, which was achieved by immersing the panels in a boiling caustic cyanide solution bath – a process which is not available today! The unpainted bonnets gave improved heat transfer and avoided the problem of the early enamel paints discolouring with the engine heat. Most restored appliances of this type now use Chrysler Sapphire Blue metallic paint as an alternative.

The engine inside of SN 1549 is a derivative of the engine used in subsidy lorries produced during the First World War (owners of such vehicles were given a government subsidy of £110 if it complied with the War Office specification and could be called upon for military use). The engine has fewer components than the earlier model, which had separate cylinders and features conventional wet sump lubrication and only single spark plugs per cylinder. Ignition is by an impulse magneto. On this type of magneto the input shaft is coupled by a clock spring arrangement which winds up as the starting handle is turned and then releases quickly at the point of ignition. This increases the speed of the armature of the magneto, resulting in a stronger spark; however, the inherent dangers of kickback are still present.

At the rear of the engine there is a massive flywheel into which the cone clutch is fitted. Compared with a conventional plate clutch, a cone clutch has a far more two-state action, either being engaged or disengaged. Fully disengaging the clutch moves the clutch drum into contact with a pad of sprungloaded friction material, which slows down the gearbox input shaft to assist gear changing. The gearbox does not have synchromesh, so the process of double de-clutching is essential if smooth noise-free gear changes are to be effected. In this process the clutch is depressed (disengaged) and the gear lever moved into neutral. The clutch is then momentarily released (engaged), which forces the transmission shafts to match the engine speed before the clutch is depressed once more as the new gear selection is made.

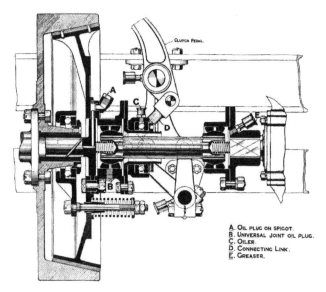

A. Oil plug on spigot.
B. Universal joint oil plug.
C. Oiler.
D. Connecting link.
E. Greaser.

The engine is coupled to the gearbox through the power takeoff. This is an arrangement of gears which transfers the engine power to the main water pump when the engagement lever is pulled. Universal joints or even flexible couplings had yet to be common automotive practice, so Dennis used box joints of their own design: a square of steel with bevelled sides located into a box of similar size. This enables the engine power to be transferred smoothly even though the shafts may not be perfectly concentric. To eliminate steel-to-steel contact, bronze slippers are interposed between the faces. When the whole assembly is packed with grease, a coupling with only a small amount of backlash is achieved. Excessive wear on the box joint is clearly indicated by the large amount of grease flung from it when the engine is running.

The larger-engined 60 hp Dennis N Type was the popular choice if a wheeled escape was to be carried. The Bass Brewery of Burton upon Trent purchased their Dennis in 1921 and kept it until 1963, when it was sold to a scrapyard to be cut up for metal reclamation. Fortunately it was purchased for preservation and has returned to the brewery to relive old memories. The brewery fire brigade also responded to calls from the Burton upon Trent Fire Brigade, for which they received an extra sixpence (2½ p) every time they left the confines of the brewery. It was on these occasions that the suction hose would be used to draw water from village ponds and streams, but not at the brewery. The brewery had a comprehensive array of fire hydrants that could be directly coupled into the pump.

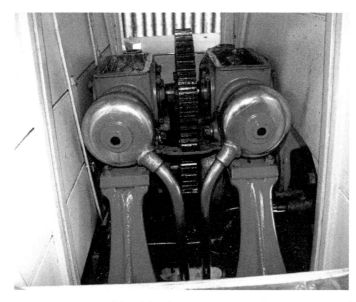

Turbine pumps are not capable of developing suction to draw water into the pump body unless they are primed. Priming the pump requires the air in the pump body to be removed, creating a partial vacuum, so that water will be forced into the pump by atmospheric air pressure. The 60 hp Dennis N Type has twin piston primers for this task. Each primer has two horizontally opposed pistons linked to a conventional crankshaft by short connecting rods. The primer is engaged by sliding a spur gear along the power takeoff shaft to engage with the matching gear on the primer. The pump on FA1075 is unusual as it is fitted with three delivery valves rather than the more common arrangement of just two deliveries. During pumping, a small flow of cold water is diverted through to the engine to keep it cool; the displaced hot water runs out of the radiator overflow. The 60 hp engines of this type were of advanced dry sump design, with the engine oil being circulated from an external oil tank (this being common practice on Formula 1 racing engines eighty years later). The oil also benefits from the circulation of cold, fresh pump-water as the tank is fitted with an intercooler. So much of the technology present on automotive engines today was present on Dennis's a hundred years ago, but formed from brass and rivets.

Chapter 2

1920–1930

DENNIS

TURBINE MOTOR
FIRE ENGINES

The latest Model 40/45 h.p. light type
300/350 Gallon Turbine Fire Engine

Telegrams : " DENNIS," GUILDFORD
Telephone : 575 (4 lines) GUILDFORD
Cables : A.B.C. 5th Edition, LIEBER'S,
BENTLEYS and MARCONI

DENNIS BROS. LTD.
Guildford, England

THE small 40/45 h.p. 300/350 gallon Turbine Fire Engine we are now offering is the result of fifteen years' experience in motor fire engine manufacture, during which time we have supplied nearly one thousand machines, which are to be found in service in all parts of the world. *The London Fire Brigade alone have over 100 Dennis Fire Engines in service.*

We are fulfilling a long felt want in producing a light motor turbine pump at a reasonable price which will come within the scope of the smaller brigades, and we invite enquiries so that a demonstration and inspection of the capabilities of this small engine can be arranged.

Sectional view of a Dennis multi-stage Turbine Fire Pump, complete with exhauster pumps. (Patent No. 146208)

The 1920s saw the dropping of the Gwynne turbine pump in favour of a fire-fighting water pump manufactured by Dennis. The pump was based on an existing design by Tamini of Italy and was initially described with Dennis Tamini patents. The Tamini connection was soon forgotten and a range of three Dennis pumps emerged, simply designated Dennis Nos 1, 2 or 3. The No. 1 pump was primarily used for trailer pumps driven by a single-cylinder engine, while Nos 2 and 3 were used on appliances. The pumping capabilities were primarily limited by the input power, with the No. 2 pump being capable of 500 gallons per minute and the No. 3 pump 1,000 gallons per minute in extremis. A clever design feature of the pump was that high-pressure water was present on both sides of the impeller so that there was no axial thrust on the turbine shaft. Dennis were proud to declare in their advertising for this pump that at the great fire of Thessalonika (Greece, 1917), a Dennis fire engine established a record for pumping seawater onto the blaze non-stop for seventeen days. It escaped notice that the appliance was actually fitted with the preceding Gwynne pump!

In 1926, a far greater revolution was to emerge from the Dennis factory. Gone were the separate power train components mounted on a sub-chassis contained with the main chassis rails, to be replaced by a unit construction engine complete with an electric starter motor. Even the power takeoff for the fire-fighting water pump was integral to the new gearbox. Externally, the appliance looked conventional. This example was supplied new to the Benoni Fire Brigade on the outskirts of Johannesburg in 1927. The small rear locker behind the main hose locker no longer contained the pump primers as the machine was fitted with the new Dennis No. 2 pump. Instead the locker was dedicated to hold the SAFOAM charges for the chemical extinguishers that were carried either side of the pump.

Today, the SAFOAM chemical extinguishers have been replaced by conventional soda-acid extinguishers. The original factory photograph was taken on the streets of Dennisville, an area of Guildford where the factory built housing for its employees. In the background you can see the rooves of the vehicle errecting sheds. Dennisville still exists today, although the old factory has now virtually been demolished to make way for a business park built during the 1990s.

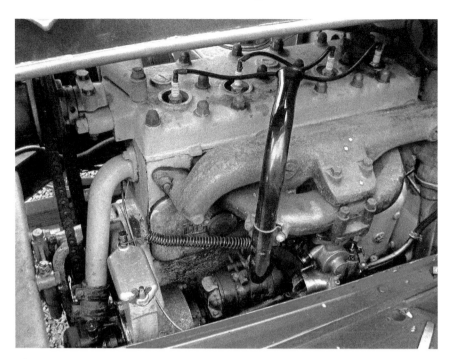

The engine is a monoblock side-valve design with a capacity of 3 litres. It has a very small single block one piece iron casting. Ignition is by magneto only. A small 6-volt starter motor is capable of turning the engine over with a good turn of speed so that starting is reliable. A dynamo of similar size keeps the battery charged. The petrol tank is mounted high up on the scuttle in front of the driver, with the fuel being simply gravity fed into the float chamber of the carburettor. The radiator header and bottom tanks are cast in gunmetal (copper 88 per cent, tin 10 per cent, zinc 2 per cent) to resist corrosion from sea water as the fire-fighting pump still passes water through the engine to provide cooling during pumping. On this machine the water circulation pump impeller was completely corroded away as an aluminum type had been fitted in error.

In 1928 the first unit construction Dennis, which was termed the '250 Gallon Model', was uprated to the G Type. Again, it was based around the 30-cwt commercial chassis. Pneumatic tyres were fitted as standard and always included a spare wheel, although solid tyres were still available as an option. A more stylised tapered bonnet surrounded the deep radiator. For the first time the starting handle passed through the radiator core. Although the G Type was fitted with an electric starter, the ability to start by hand cranking would still be considered essential right up to the 1960s.

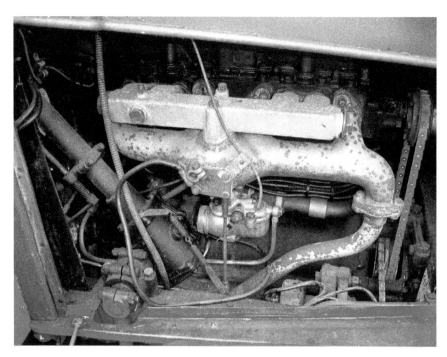

The engine for the G Type was an updated version of the earlier engine used in the 250 gallon model. An overhead valve cylinder head gave increased power. White & Poppe, the original engine supplier to Dennis, expanded from a staff of 300 to 12,000 during the First World War with a factory covering 67 acres on the outskirts of Coventry. Post-war, the factory struggled to survive and was purchased by Dennis in 1919, who transferred all production to Guildford. Dennis Brothers were appointed as fire engine suppliers to George V in 1928 and this was reflected in the badging on the radiator.

The end of the 1920s saw the last evolution of the Dennis N Type in the form of the 'low load' chassis. This was the concept of an appliance where it was easy for the firemen to clamber on board, and gave excellent road holding due to the low centre of gravity. Fifty years later, all of these characteristics were applied to the Dennis Rapier. This machine cost £1,485 new (equivalent to £85,000 today) and operated with the Burton upon Trent Fire Brigade until 1952, when it was sold to the Bass Brewery Fire Brigade at Burton. This machine attended the Great Fauld Explosion in 1944, when a munitions store ignited and resulted in the largest non-nuclear explosion ever recorded. The key factor which enabled the low ride height to be achieved was the mounting of the engine in the separate sub-chassis at a steep angle, which is most noticeable when the bonnet covers are raised.

The fire-fighting water pump is a Dennis No. 3, capable of delivering 1,000 gallons of water per minute. To enable this rate to be achieved it must be connected to its water source by 6-inch diameter suction hose. Three lengths of this hose are carried in the centre of the body above the hose locker. This appliance saw the first appearance of the standard pumping system which would remain unchanged for the next fifty years. The pump could be fed either from a hydrant, open water or from the machines own internal water tank. Although the output normally went to hoses connected to the pump deliveries, it could also be directed through to the hose reel. All combinations of pump operation were controlled by a five-way valve that gave the following possibilites: hydrant to tank; hydrant to hose reel; tank to pump to hose reel; hydrant to pump to hose reel; all off.

Due to the low-mounted fuel tank, petrol could no longer be supplied to the Zenith carburettor by gravity feed. A device called a Hydrovac, which relied on engine suction from the inlet manifold, pulled petrol through to a small auxillary petrol tank mounted on the scuttle, which then fed the carburettor by gravity. Mechanical and electric petrol pumps were still many years in the future. The White & Poppe engine now carried all the engine oil in a conventional sump rather than using an external oil tank. The oil filler cap was mounted just ahead of the engine's water pump. Ignition was by a conventional distributor, points and coil, supplemented by a magneto. An electric starter motor provided rapid starting, although drain cocks, which allowed petrol to be poured easily into the engine to assist starting, were still fitted to each cylinder. The engine power was transmitted through a cone clutch which had remained unchanged in design from 1908. Flexible fibre couplings now replaced the box joints and the gearbox now featured an integral power takeoff.

The low-load concept was also seen on three unique appliances for the New Zealand Fire Service. Based on the Dennis Dart bus chassis of that period, it was fitted with the Light Six overhead-valve engine. It was supplied new to the Dunedin Fire Brigade and, although thirteenth in their fleet, it was identified as Dunedin 14 to avoid the possible assignment of bad luck. The Dennis Dart name was reapplied to a bus chassis in the 1990s, and once again a small number of fire appliances were built on this chassis type.

Chapter 3

1930–1940

BY APPOINTMENT
TO H.M. THE KING

PATENT TURBINE
MOTOR FIRE ENGINES

**THE DENNIS LOW-LOAD 650/800 GALLON MODEL
WITH VACUUM-SERVO 4-WHEEL BRAKES AND
PUMP IN CENTRAL POSITION**

Telegrams: DENNIS, GUILDFORD
Telephone: 1575 (6 lines) GUILDFORD
Codes: A.B.C. 5th Edition, LIEBER'S,
    BENTLEYS and MARCONI

DENNIS BROS., LTD.,
Guildford, England
Motor Vehicle Manufacturers to H.M. The King.

The 1930s introduced a new range of models with none of the previous decades models carried over. Evocative names such as the Ace, Big Six and Big Four were now used as a descriptive name to enhance their capability. All of the smaller capacity appliances were based around the Dennis A/C Type four-cylinder engine. The Dennis Ace was primarily a Braidwood-bodied machine where as before, the crew sat on top of the hose locker box. The Ace had the front wheels set back from the engine so that there was a prounced overhang at the front. Very soon after its introduction this model was christened the Flying Pig, owing to its looks!

The A Type engine was a compact four-cylinder side-valve unit of 3,770cc, developing 60 bhp – a very modest amount of power by today's standards to propel a laden vehicle of 5 tons. Dual ignition with two spark plugs per cylinder was fitted, with one set fed by a conventional coil and the second set by magneto. The petrol is pumped to the carburettor by a mechanical fuel pump located at the base of the engine. As overheating, which plagues this engine, causes the petrol to vaporise in the long feed pipe, it was often wrapped in asbestos tape to minimise heat conduction. The 1930s also saw the introduction of hydraulically operated brakes. Transmitting stopping power to brakes on the front wheels was now simple as flexible rubber hoses could be used to carry the hydraulic fluid from the master cylinder mounted externally on the chassis rail through to the brake cylinders.

Although most Dennis Aces which were built between 1933 and 1939 had Braidwood bodies, a small number had limousine-style bodies. A notable surviving example is the one which was first supplied to the Sonning and Mortimer Fire Brigade at the start of 1938. The body was made by Markhams of Reading, who specialised in producing sport-style bodies on ash frames for such makes as Bentley. This is reflected in stylish rear treatment of the body as it flows into the pump bay and the extravagant design of the suction hose compartments so that they are fully integrated into the body.

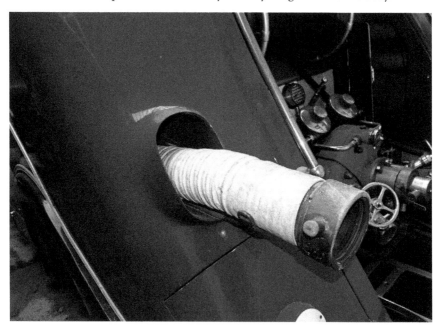

At the start of the 1930s the large Dennis pumping appliance was known as the 80 hp (horse power) model, but soon the more evocative and descriptive names began to emerge. The 80 hp migrated to the Big Six on account of the six-cylinder side-valve engine. West Ham Fire Brigade took the first of this type in 1930, followed by a second almost identical machine a year later. They were specified with 60-foot Bailey escape ladders. This was the first Dennis that used a mid-mounted pump rather than a rear-mounted pump, which meant that pumping could begin immediately when arriving at a fire without the need to ship the escape to gain access to the pump controls. The unpainted wooden bodywork has survived exceptionally well over the past eighty years despite standing out in the open for a number of years.

The engine has a single-piece cast-iron block mounted on an aluminium crankcase. Three separate cylinder heads are used, which are interchangeable with those fitted to the four-cylinder engine used in the Ace and Light Four. The compression ratio is very low at 4:1, making the engine easy to turn over using the starting handle. Again, dual iginiton is used to ensure that starting is always possible. Lead acid accumulators (batteries) had still not achieved a level of reliability that would give confidence to dispense with the manual starting handle and magneto ignition. Located at the right end of the inlet manifold is a vacuum pipe that is connected to the brake servo. Power-assisted brakes were a welcome addition to appliances of this type, which weighed up to 6 tons when fully laden.

The City of York Big Six exhibited a new feature to Dennis fire engines. Gone was the glint of brass which required hours of polishing to maintain its shine, replaced by a maintenance-free chrome-plated finish. The instrument layout of the York machine illustrates this perfectly, where the ignition switch covers in plain brass are tarnished and dull, while the chrome-plated windscreen brackets shine. Dennis were particularly adapt at producing variations to their standard designs to suit the requirements of their customers. This Big Six has a forward-mounted ladder gantry to carry a heavy 60-foot wheeled escape dating from 1911, which the brigade wished to reuse.

Big Sixes were not confined only to pumping appliances. The same configuration, although with a longer wheel base, was used on a turntable fire engine supplied to the Belfast Fire Brigade in 1931. The German company Magirus manufactured the all-steel turntable ladder. In earlier years the ladder sections of turntable ladders were wooden, following the pattern of wheeled escape ladders. Elevation, rotation and extension were now fully powered operations through clutches, gears and winch drums. Although pneumatic tyres were common at this time, the brigade decided to still opt for solid rubber tyres in the belief that they were more robust for such a heavy vehicle. CZ503 appeared at the Hamberlin's farm auction in 2004. The top sections of the ladder had been removed many years earlier after they had buckled and collapsed while extended.

The Dennis Light Six was introduced in 1935 as a six-cylinder variant of the Dennis Ace. It was fitted with the Dennis six-cylinder overhead-cam engine in a lightweight chassis with a wheelbase of 12 feet 6 inches. Although most of the eighty-four produced went into the home market and were bodied by Dennis, those supplied overseas had bodies constructed by local bodybuilders. This Light Six was supplied new to the Christchurch Fire Brigade in New Zealand in 1937. An original feature is the unpainted bonnet made from sheet steel, which has been chemically 'blued' in a boiling caustic cyanide bath. The advantage of such a bonnet was to enable heat to transfer more quickly away from the engine and to improve the cosmetic appearance, as the oil-based paints of this era discoloured markedly when heated.

The achievements of the Dennis engine shop of the 1930s, which evolved from the takeover of White & Poppe, is often overlooked and seldom recorded. Their output included four- and six-cylinder side-valve engines, four- and six-cylinder overhead-valve engines, and this six-cylinder overhead-cam engine. The four-cylinder C Type engine from this period was still in production in 1960 in the D variant form, being used in the F30. As with all large petrol engines, overheating was a common occurrence. The Christchurch Light Six has an extra-deep radiator core to help alleviate this problem. Engines for the Dennis bus range were diesel designs, and some even featured four-valve cylinder heads, which were only to be seen in widespread use fifty years later.

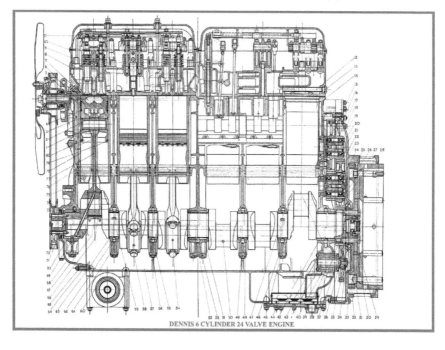

DENNIS 6 CYLINDER 24 VALVE ENGINE

The Dennis Light Four shared many of the components of the Dennis Ace, but used a more conventional chassis resulting in a longer wheelbase. Pressed steel panels were used on this example for the doors and scuttle rather than hand-formed panels. The dash panel was also a single-piece pressing. The gearbox has five gears, with the fifth gear used as an overdrive for comfortable cruising at speeds in excess of 50 mph. Even today the speedo needle can move off the dial on downhill sections of motorway roads. The lever to the left of the gearchange engages the main pump drive, while the lever to the right selects a small gear pump to feed the hosereel. 50 gallons of water are carried in the water tank.

Semi-limousine-bodied examples of the Light Four still exist. Rather than the fire crew riding on the outside of the appliance, they now had the opportunity to sit in the dry and warmth of a fully enclosed cab. This was a welcome feature as this appliance, seen here at Guildford prior to despatch, was destined for Elgin Fire Brigade in the north of Scotland. It was accepted into the National Fire Service in July 1943 and was unusual as it retained its red livery rather than being repainted NFS grey. The headlamps were fitted with blackout shutters to avoid attracting enemy bombers and white edging to the wings made the appliance more visible to passing traffic in the darkness of the war years.

The most common variant of the Light Four had the New World body style. The Braidwood-bodied appliances, where the crew rode on the outside precariously perched on the locker box holding on with only one hand to a support rail, became increasingly unsafe as road speeds increased. The New World design had the crew facing inwards to give little opportunity to them being thrown off during cornering. The reconstruction of this New World body clearly illustrates the coach-built nature of fire engines, where a hardwood frame (usually ash, or in later years Iroko from the west coast of Africa) is clad in a hand-formed steel or aluminium skin.

The Dennis Big Four was a heavyweight version of the Light Four. With a maximum running weight of almost 8 tons, it had a 3 ton greater carrying capacity of the Light Four. The engine was an all-new overhead valve design of 6.8 litres, resulting in a power output of 100 hp. Big Fours were constucted with all body styles: Braidwood, New World, semi-limousine and limousine. The Big Four was preceded by the D3, which had all the characteristics of the Big Four apart from the engine, which was a four-cylinder side-valve design, similar in concept to the A/C type engine used in the Ace and Light Four. The factory demonstrator for the Big Four style was a D3 registered BPB644. This machine was fitted with extra chrome and had unique features such as the locker door handles engraved with the Dennis name. An outstanding image of this machine shows the Prince of Wales, soon to become Edward VIII, being taken on a demonstration run.

In 1936, with the duties of the Big Four demonstrator being complete, this appliance was sold to the Long Eaton Fire Brigade. An exciting photograph shows it in attendance at a school blaze. BPB644 has survived and is now in preservation and undergoing restoration. The large headlights are mounted on swivel and tilt brackets so that they can be used as floodlights during night-time incidents.

Chapter 4

1940–1950

400/500 GALLON
FIRE ENGINES

ON THE DENNIS

CHASSIS

DENNIS BROS LTD GUILDFORD ENGLAND

PUBLICATION NO. 198C(R)

Form 44—1000/2/43

DENNIS BROS. LTD.

Order No. *50963*   Chassis Card No. *3161 A.*

Supplied to *Merryweather Etc,*   Date *March 3-1944*

W.P.O. No.

Chassis No. *3161 A*   Type *Magirus 8 Ton FE.*   Engine No. *75230*

Body No.   Type *TTL*   Series No. *Meadows 6EX*

Pump No.   No. of Cylrs. *6*   Bore *110*   Stroke. *140*

F. Axle No.   R. Axle No.

Gear Box No.

Special Details of Chassis :—

The war years saw only a limited quantity of fire engines built at Dennis. Production was concentrated on Churchill tanks (700), Army lorries (4,500), Tracked carriers (3,000) and Trailer pumps (7,000). One exception was a modest fire engine production run of forty-three turntable ladder appliances for the National Fire Service. These were fitted with the Merryweather 100-foot mechanically operated ladder. Pre-war turntable ladders were fitted with the German-manufactured Magirus ladders, which were now no longer available. It is interesting to note that on the order for these appliances they were still referred to as the Magirus Type. The ladder is directly operated by a power takeoff from the engine, with three clutches to control the motion. The ladder rotates through a gear ring on the periphery of the turntable and is elevated by screw jacks positioned either side of the ladder. Ladder extension is through a mechanical winch drum.

GXA 95 Dennis was initially allocated to the West Riding of Yorkshire region and spent the war years stationed at Goole. When the National Fire Service was disbanded in 1948 and control given back to the various local authorities, chassis 3161A became the property of the West Riding of Yorkshire Fire Brigade. Operating out of Goole until 1951, it was transferred to Keighley and remained in service there for another eighteen years. After a brief spell in storage, the Dennis was bought by Grimsby Fire Brigade as a stopgap replacement while one of its more modern appliances was being repaired. GLW 424, formerly with the Bristol Fire Brigade, has had a less fortunate life. After standing out in the open for many years there is considerable deterioration. Significant engine components are missing, which make an engine replacement almost inevitable. It is now in preservation with GXA 95.

A description of the wartime production at the Dennis factory would not be complete without mention of the Dennis trailer pump. Designed to be towed behind a van or large car, it was the backbone of the fire service, controlling fires created by German bombing raids. Fitted with the well-proven engine used in the Ace and Light Four fire engines, which was directly coupled to the Dennis No. 2 fire pump, it could run for days on end with little or no intervention. Starting was by hand crank only, without any battery or electrical system apart from the impulse magneto. Dennis had manufactured trailer pumps even during the First World War to pump out the trenches in France, and in peacetime promoted them for the safe guarding of country estates. This type had a single-cylinder JAP engine and a small Dennis No. 1 fire pump.

This appliance is equipped with:—
An 11 in. searchlight, a detachable
draw-bar, first-aid apparatus com-
prising 150 ft. hose and a 40-gallon
tank, used in conjunction with the
main pump.

ROWNTREE & Cº Lᵈ
FIRE BRIGADE
YORK

When Chocolate is off the ration
Fire will still be controlled . . .

The immediate post-war years saw the start of a new generation of Dennis fire engines designated the F series. Starting with the F1 and running through to F131 thirty years later, this was a very successful range of appliances which embodied the characteristics that every chief fire officer desired. Not all F numbers were used, some being allocated to prototypes which never reached production. Announced in 1947, the F1 was a development of the pre-war Light Four. There was indecision as to whether it should have a name apart from its type allocation. Early publicity material hinted that internally it was called the Onslow. It had an improved version of the small Dennis four-cylinder. Two body styles were available as standard. Rowntrees of York took delivery of a New World-style F1, which Dennis capitalised on in their advertisements. Those brigades requiring the F1 to carry an escape ladder were offered the Braidwood-bodied variant.

The Dennis F1 was followed by the F2 in 1948. This was a larger machine with a 13-foot 6-inch wheelbase and a width of 7 feet. For the first time the new Rolls-Royce B80 eight-cylinder engine was used which produced 150 hp – twice as much as that developed by the F1. Dennis emphasised the high power-to-weight ratio and the gearbox with close ratios to give rapid acceleration. Both mid- and rear-mounted pump body styles were available. Styling was also a concept being introduced by the design department rather than functionality being totally dominant.

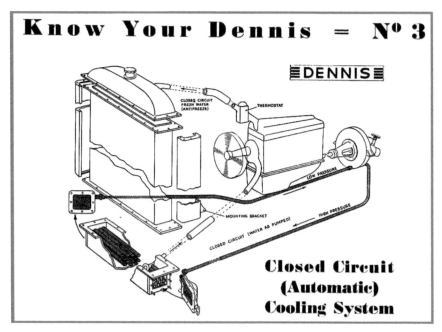

A new innovation was applied to the engine cooling system. For the first time a proportion of the pumped water was not passed directly to the engine to keep it cool during pumping operations. Instead, a heat exchanger was used which recirculated the water back to the pump, leaving the the engine cooling water uncontaminated. The use of a closed-circuit cooling system meant that anti-freeze could be used and salt water pumping did not require the flushing of the engine with water from a hydrant after use. Dennis were very aware that sales success could be achieved by promoting their technical advancements. Publications such as the *Fire Protection Review*, which were everyday reading in all fire stations, carried a series of 'Know Your Dennis' advertisements which both educated the fireman and extolled the virtues of the technology in new Dennises.

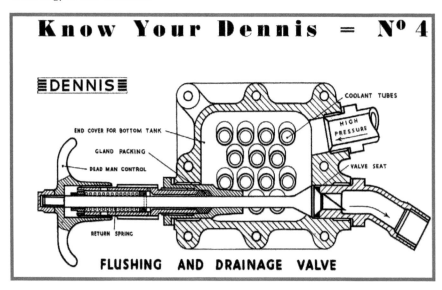

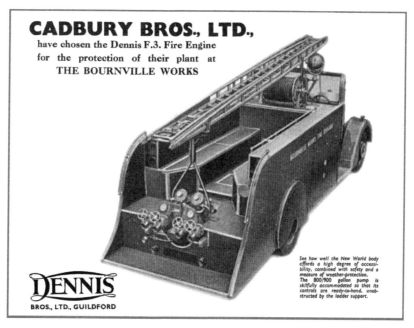

CADBURY BROS., LTD.,
have chosen the Dennis F.3. Fire Engine
for the protection of their plant at
THE BOURNVILLE WORKS

See how well the New World body affords a high degree of accessibility, combined with safety and a measure of weather-protection. The 800/900 gallon pump is skilfully accommodated so that its controls are ready-to-hand, unobstructed by the ladder support.

DENNIS
BROS., LTD., GUILDFORD

The F3 was slightly larger than the F2 with the wheelbase increasing to 13 feet 11 inches. It was introduced as a lower-cost F2 primarily aimed at the overseas markets of the Commonwealth countries. A six-cylinder Meadows engine was used, which gave 125 hp and enabled the Dennis No. 3 pump to achieve 960 gallons per minute at a water pressure of 80 lbs per square inch. Despite the increased pumping capability of the No. 3 pump, it was not automatically fitted with four delivery valves. This was an option to be specified by the customer. Not to be outdone by their rival chocolate maker Rowntree, Cadbury took delivery of an F3 in 1948. As with many works fire appliances only a small number of miles were covered, so the chance of survival into preservation was improved. The Cadbury F3 is one such lucky survivor.

Chapter 5

1950–1960

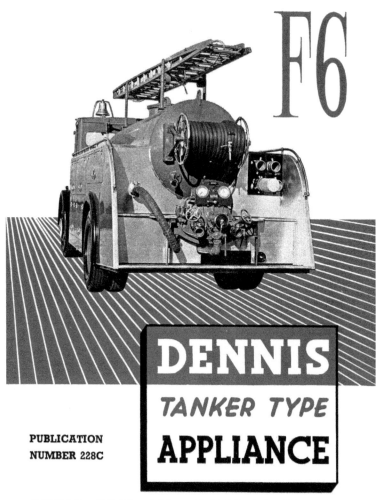

F6

DENNIS

TANKER TYPE

APPLIANCE

PUBLICATION
NUMBER 228C

DENNIS   BROS   LTD   GUILDFORD   ENGLAND

The Dennis F6 was based on the F1 and retained the same four-cylinder Dennis engine. The principal feature of this appliance was the 600-gallon water tank. In many developing countries a mains water supply was not available, so all the water for fire-fighting purposes had to be transported to the scene of the fire. In addition to its fire-fighting use, Dennis were keen to stress its multi-function capability. A sparge bar (a bar fitted with sprinkler heads) could be located under the front bumper for street-washing purposes! In addition, the power of the Dennis No. 2 pump was emphasised as being ideal for clearing blocked drains and gullies. Such versatility appealed to municipal authorities where their remit extended to both highway maintenance and the provision of fire cover.

The most significant Dennis of the 1950s was the Dennis F8. Launched in 1950 as the Ulster variant, Dennis advertising proclaimed:

> The new Ulster model-series F8 fire engine is a small appliance designed for work in confined areas or in rural districts where high speed and manoeuvrability are essentials of effective operation. No appliance could be more compact. The Ulster provides limousine accomodation for a full crew and equipment, carries a 35ft extension ladder, a 500 gpm main pump and 200 gallons of water.

A series of advertisements in the *Fire Prevention Review* kept pressing home this message.

SQUEEZE IT THROUGH

With an overall width of only 6 ft. 6 in. this new appliance is 12 in. slimmer than standard

TURN IT ROUND

A really short wheelbase of 10 ft. gives a turning circle of approximately 36 ft.

TAKE IT UNDER

Maximum head room required with an extension ladder is only 9 ft. 6 in.

The F8 was a very popular appliance and many have survived into preservation. It is powered by six-cylinder Rolls-Royce B60 engine of 4.25 litres producing 120 hp. The controls for operating the pump are very simple. The left lever engages a clutch to connect the priming pumps when it is neccessary to draw water through the suction hose into the pump. For turbine pumps to operate it is necessary that they are first full of water and without the presence of any air. The right lever controls the speed of the engine, which drives the pump through a power takeoff. A progression in the development of the pump is that it is now no longer necessary to manually operate the air valve which connects the priming pumps to the body of the main pump. This is now performed automatically by a cable-operated mechanism when the primer clutch is engaged.

Dennis F8s came in many configurations. As well as having the standard enclosed crew cab, RUM 970 provided access to a New World body seating arrangement through sliding doors. A crew of ten could therefore be carried at the loss of the main 300 gallon water tank. However, two tanks of 50 gallons each are located under the rear seats to give some immediate response capability. Although the majority of F8s had bodies constructed by the Dennis factory, some were built by Alfred Miles Ltd of Cheltenham. The body shape was radically different with roller shutter doors covering the lockers. Although originally fitted with only a bell to warn oncoming traffic of the presence of a fire engine, two-tone horns, which can be seen behind the front grill, were later added by the Northumberland Fire Brigade who operated ten of these appliances.

The Dennis F.8 is rapidly becoming first favourite amongst Industrial Brigades by virtue of its great manœuvrability—its speed off the mark and steady pumping ability.

Accompanying illustrations show the great Works of Singer Sewing Machine Co. Ltd., Clydebank, and the Dennis F.8 recently added to their Brigade's strength.

With a 120 h.p. 6-cyl. Rolls-Royce Engine and the famous Dennis 500 g.p.m. Turbine Pump with new horizontal primer, the F.8 is unsurpassed in versatility and performance.

The photographs above are reproduced by kind permission of the Singer Sewing Machine Co. Ltd., Clydebank.

DENNIS ('F' SERIES)
HIGH PERFORMANCE FIRE ENGINES

Due to their small size and manouevrabiity the F8 was ideal for the large post-war industrial complexes. The Singer sewing machine factory on Clydebank had a workforce of 16,000 during the 1960s, with a factory covering more ground than many small towns. Purchased in 1955, the Singer F8 still exists today in preservation. The aluminium-framed opening front windows have been replaced by fixed rubber strip glazed windows following an accident. A precursor to rotating blue warning beacons were amber lights, located above the front windows. As flashing turn signal lights replaced the trafficator arms (which DSN 175 still has) the hot wire flasher unit, now commonly available, could also be used to make the amber warning lights flash.

After the war the Home Office prepared specifications for the minimum requirements which fire engines should satisfy. In response to this, in 1949 Dennis introduced the F7, the first of which (DHM 727) was supplied to East Ham Fire Brigade. This machine used the eight-cylinder Rolls-Royce engine as used in the F2 to give a top speed of over 60 mph and the ability to accelerate to 40 mph in under 30 seconds. For a fire engine weighing 8 tons fully laden, this was a dramatic performance in 1950. Seventy F7s were built to be followed by the F12 and F15, which differed only in detail. The pump was generally mid-mounted. The preserved Nottingham Fire Brigade F12 is an example of the rear-mounted pump variant.

Mounting the pump at the rear gave more locker space. Weight was also saved as the suction and delivery pipes were not duplicated leading to either side of the appliance. However, access to the pump was severely restricted, which meant that before pumping could commence the escape ladder would have to be shipped. F12s and their variants were not just confined to pump escapes. Shown posing outside the Dennis factory bicycle sheds is a very elegant open machine destined for Cape Town. South African fire brigades continued to prefer open appliances in this style for the next thirty years.

Three F12s were built as emergency tenders, two of which survive today. VVC 898 was first registered in May 1958 and was one of the last F12s to be built. It is equipped with a large electrical generator to provide lighting at incidents and to power electrically operated cutting tools. Supplied to the City of Coventry Fire Brigade in red, it was later resprayed with Coventry Yellow to increase the visibility when viewed under sodium street lighting. In 1974, upon transference to the newly formed West Midlands Fire Brigade, it was again resprayed back to red and was designated a breathing apparatus control unit. After being withdrawn from service in 1980 in excellent condition it was given to the Fire Service Museum Trust, from which time it should have had a safe and secure life in preservation. However, it was allowed to deteriorate, standing outside exposed to the elements for a considerable time. It was during this period that much of it was taken apart, never to be reassembled. Finally, its future was secured in 2014. Through the flaking red paintwork the Coventry Yellow can still be seen.

The turntable ladder fire engines of the 1950s were based on the F14, F17 and F21 chassis. All had a wheelbase of 15 feet 6 inches, with only minor improvements on each model variant. EJV 955 was supplied new to the Grimsby Fire Brigade in 1954. Now that hostilities had ended with Germany, Metz ladders were once more available and these were used by Dennis. The ladder is a four-section all-steel construction and extends 30 m (100 feet). The cab design was unusual in that the crew section faces rearwards and is exposed to the elements. A sliding window in the rear of the cab wall enabled messages to be passed between the driver and the crew!

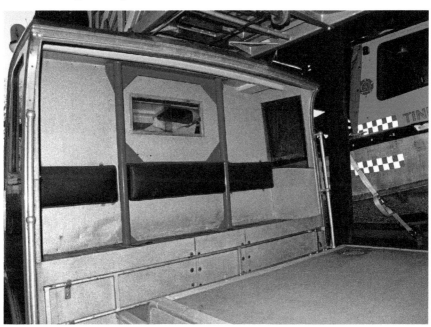

OZ 9607 was also built in 1954 for the Northern Ireland Fire Brigade but featured the five-section 125-foot Metz ladder. The fifth section of the ladder was quite flexible and in the 1960s a decision was made to remove the top section as extension past 100 feet was seldom used. During the period of Troubles in Northern Ireland, when sectarian violence against any representation of authority was frequent, the exposed crew section was enclosed with additional doors for entrance. When OZ 9607 came out of service the internal bomb blast screens were still fitted to the windows. The Rochdale F21 is the only surviving example of a 125-foot Metz ladder in the UK.

The ladder operator either leans over the deck or crouches on the deck as the ladder is rotated. A tubular horizontal ring acccessible from any position controls the engine throttle to vary the speed of the ladder operations. The hand levers select the elevation, extension and rotation functions through clutches which transmit the drive from the engine to the winch drums and rotation gear. A large circular plumb bob weight automatically controls the plumbing of the ladder. Ladder plumbing maintains the altitude of the ladder when the appliance is parked on a slope. The distance that the ladder could safely be extended depends on the angle of the ladder. An extension of 125 feet can only be achieved at the maximum inclination of 75 degrees.

Many of the F17 turntable ladder appliances were also fitted with the Dennis No. 3 pump mounted centrally in the chassis. Prior to the ladder being elevated, it is necessary to engage the axle locks which compress the rear suspension springs to provide stability. Engagement of the axle locks releases the four mechanical jacks. Wooden pads carried in the rear lockers may be placed under the jacks to spread the load on weak or uneven surfaces. The ability of the Dennis body shop to produce elegant designs to match the requirement of the customer is well illustrated by this F17 supplied to a South African Fire Brigade. Virtually all F17s were built as TLs. OZ 9606, the sister machine to OZ 9607, was an exception. It was configured as an emergency tender, but unusually it was also fitted with a mid-mounted pump. A long overhang behind the rear wheels exaggerated the magnificence of its proportion.

Chapter 6

1960–1970

'D'SERIES

DENNIS

Publication No. NS.1140/R

The F26 was introduced in the late 1950s but continued in manufacture for many years after. It was a large appliance and featured many of the attributes of the F12 in a modern styling package for the period: TSA 980 is a fine example. The most noticeable feature is the unpainted body covered in Stucco-patterned aluminium sheet, with a painted front panel and roof. The firemaster of the North-Eastern Brigade (Scotland) was very particular in specifying every detail of this machine, for which he wished to pay £5,074 less a £76 discount as the brigade would supply the alternator! The pump fitted to the rear of the machine was a Dennis No. 2 pump, capable of delivering 600 gallons per minute.

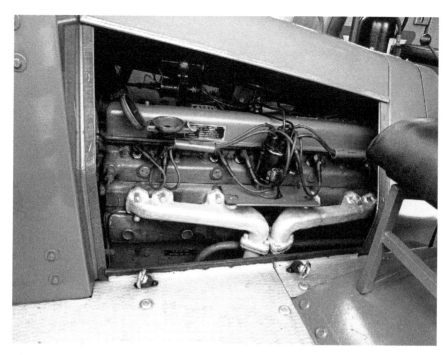

The engine in the F26 was the well-proven Rolls-Royce B80 petrol engine, in this instance developing 160 hp. The twin ignition coils are retained, as on the earlier F-series machines, as are the dual petrol pumps. Both a mechanical and electric petrol pump were fitted with a changeover switch located under the engine cover. The electric pump was a twin solenoid SU type which makes a characteristic ticking sound as each stroke of the pump lifts the fuel from the petrol tank and forces it forwards to the carburettor. The F26 was fitted with a 23-gallon tank, giving a range of often no more than 120 miles.

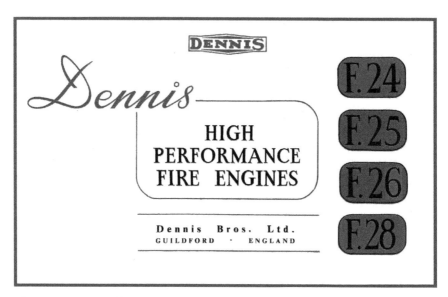

The F26 was part of a range of similar looking appliances. The F24 featured the eight-cylinder Rolls-Royce engine coupled to a Rolls automatic gearbox. An automatic gearbox was a new feature and marked a further progression in the development of the Dennis fire engine. Both the F24 and F26 (manual gearbox) had a 12-foot 3-inch wheel base. The F25 and F28 were smaller appliances with a 10-foot 9-inch wheel base. The F25 was fitted with the low-cost Dodge KEW2 six-cylinder engine. This appliance was soon replaced by the F28, which had the latest Rolls-Rocye B61 engine, giving over 30 per cent more power. Dennis always emphasised the high performance capabilities of their machines with the understanding that the very best always costs a little more. The F27 designation was used for the turntable ladder version.

In this view of the Dennis body shop, five of the F24–28 series appliances are under construction along with a refuse collection lorry. The body shop was about to undergo a significant change in production technique as Dennis moved into the use of glass-reinforced plastic (GRP) rather than handcrafted steel and aluminium panels. The F36 (eight-cylinder) and the F38 (six-cylinder) featured the new moulded front panels. MTU 317H is a late model F38 with a dedicated panel section below the radiator cap for the large cast aluminium letters spelling out D-E-N-N-I-S.

Until the late 1950s, Dennis had not considered that diesel engines offered sufficient performance for their fire appliances. However, with the widespread acceptance of the Rolls-Royce C6 diesel engine the first diesel engined appliance appeared. For the next twenty years diesel-engined appliances would be manufactured alongside their petrol-engined counterparts, with F numbers running from F101 onwards. As the C6 engine was not primarily designed as a commercial vehicle engine, Dennis began to look elsewhere for diesel power plants. The diesel engine of their own manufacture was occasionally used when ultimate performance was not required, such as the F103 emergency tender. However, it was the AEC-manufactured AVU470 engine which found favour in the F106 supplied to the New Zealand Fire Brigade.

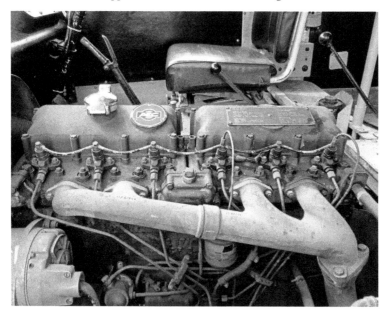

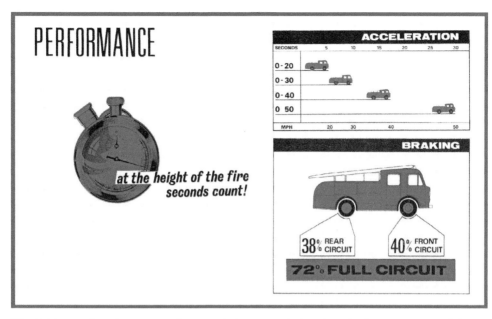

The F44 was the ultimate appliance of this period, fitted with the more powerful B81 eight-cylinder engine developing 235 hp and coupled to an Allison fully automatic transmisssion. The Allison auto gearbox would remain with Dennis to the end of fire engine production. The Dennis brochures of the day declared, 'The F44 combines excellent acceleration, a high top speed, and traditional Dennis handling qualities with unrivalled ease of driving control. These outstanding features make the F44 the finest most advanced fire-fighting vehicle of its type available anywhere in the world.' The cutaway illustration shows the adoption of some of the modern technology which was now available. Disk brakes are now fitted to the front wheels (although these were ahead of their time and did not appear again for another twenty-five years) and the bell is supplemented by two-tone air horns.

The F107 chassis was primarily used as a chassis for emergency tenders. EBB 783C was supplied new to the Newcastle and Gateshead Fire Brigade and was delivered in maroon with post office red highlights on the wings and lockers. Silver lettering and pin striping set off the unique colour scheme. Twin bells, one set of air horns and a small rotating blue beacon provide warning to the oncoming traffic. In 1974 it became part of the Tyne and Wear Metropolitan Fire Brigade and was withdrawn from service after being on the run for twenty years. There are two power takeoffs, one for the Broughton hydraulic winch and the second for the 110-volt generator which was used to provide scene lighting at incidents. Later, enhancements replaced the single beacon with three larger beacons and a duplicate set of air horns.

Not all Dennis fire appliances were built on a dedicated fire engine chassis. The heavy recovery tender supplied to Durham County Fire Brigade in 1970 was built on the Maxim heavy goods vehicle chassis. Originally these units were powered by the Cummins V8 Vale engine, which were soon to emerge as being very unreliable. Dennis therefore switched to the Perkins V8 engine, which proved a successful power unit for all Dennis fire appliances for the next twenty years. Three engine sizes were used, with capacities of 510, 540 and 640 cubic inches (10.5 litres). The 540 cubic-inch variant was often turbocharged to provide additional power. In preservation, this appliance showed its capability when it towed home an operations support tender, complete with a vintage fire engine load!

The Dennis D Type introduced in 1967 broke away from the F series of numbering. It was promoted as the replacement for the F8 as being a small nimble appliance for both rural districts and congested city centres. To achieve a more modest cost, initially the D Type was available with only the 4.2-litre engine from the large Jaguar saloon cars of the period. With 180 hp available, this gave very good performance equal to the more expensive Rolls-Royce B61 engine. Another minor cost-saving move was the fitting of single combined main beam/dip headlights. The body was available with either hinged locker doors or roller shutter doors. Hinged locker doors enabled a more flexible layout of locker space and were more robust, but gave less access.

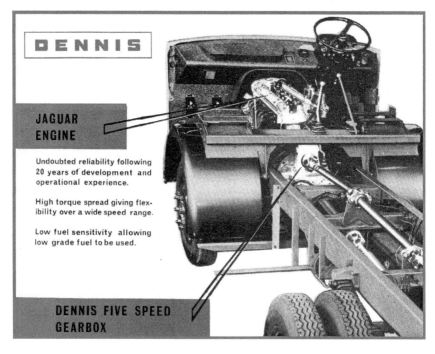

Chapter 7

1970–1980

'R' SERIES
FIRE APPLIANCES

Dennis entered the 1970s with the traditonal ash-framed F series appliances and the smaller D Type range. However, to remain competitive the factory realised that it had to move forward away from the craftsman-built fire engine to one more capable of mass production by less skilled labour. This appeared in the form of the R Type. The 'R' was initially indicative of a 'Rationalised' range of appliances, but was quickly changed to a range being suitable for 'Retained' fire stations. Retained fire stations did not have full-time manning and had a low number of call outs compared to a full-time station. The ash-framed cab was replaced by a tubular steel structure integrated into a one-piece glass fibre moulding. This was simple to manufacture and also resulted in enhanced safety in the event of a crash. The initial R type was the basis of a range of appliances with a numbering system similar to the F series.

LOW INITIAL COST
Rugged. Reliable. Ready. The 'R' could describe almost any feature of this exciting new appliance. It's new, but retains all that's best in Dennis machines – built to exacting specifications, hand finished, ready for action under the worst conditions. For all that, it comes at a competitive price that is within the reach of any brigade. The choice is exciting too: Diesel or Petrol engines, Automatic or Manual gearbox, Multi or Single pressure pumps, gunmetal or alloy.

Additionally, we'll be only too happy to discuss with you any modifications needed for your own Dennis 'R' series machine.

Water Tender Ladder

This decade also introduced the multi-pressure fire-fighting water pump to Dennis appliances. Hose reels carried either side of the appliance at the rear were quick to deploy and were more effective if fed with water at extra-high pressure. A new generation of pumps had emerged from the Coventry-based company Godiva, which provided this facility. They were used by Dennis as a replacement for their own range of pumps, which were difficult to adapt for this type of high-pressure operation. The R series also had a new styled front cab moulding which was adopted onto all models. Many of the R series were fitted with a utilitarian fabricated front bumper rather than curved chrome bumper present in the F series in order to reduce costs.

The era of the petrol-engined Dennis was coming to a close. One of the last models to feature a petrol engine was the F60, with the Rolls-Royce B81 engine and a manual gearbox. The F61 had an automatic gearbox, and in keeping with the Dennis numbering tradition (with numbers below 100 specifying petrol) the R61 was also petrol-engined with an automatic gearbox. The braking system on Dennis appliances had now advanced to air brakes. In this system, an engine-driven compressor feeding reservoir air tanks maintain a supply of high-pressure air. When the brakes are applied, the air is released into cylinders which force the brake shoes into contact with the brake drums. For safety reasons at least two air tanks were fitted, each with their own pressure gauge mounted in the instrument binnacle of the dashboard.

Rather than use a conventional chassis for turntable ladder fire appliances, Dennis produced a range of low-cab-height chassis designated as the Delta chassis. This was achieved by mounting the engine and gearbox low down behind the front axle rather than above the axle. The flexibility of Dennis to engineer solutions to meet operational needs enhanced their reputation as the leading fire engine manufacturer both in the UK and many countries of the world. The Magirus ladder used on this F123 Dennis Delta was also technically advanced. This was the first ladder which could depress well below the horizontal, making it ideal for water rescue work where the appliance may be safely parked on a river bank and extended out over the water flow.

The Magirus ladder had many uses apart from providing access to tall buildings and being used as a water tower; Tyne and Wear Metropolitan Fire Brigade used one of their turntable ladder appliances to launch their fire boat into the River Tyne. An electric winch powered by a generator carried on the deck of the appliance was used to raise and lower the boat from the river. The ladder also had the ability to carry a two-man cage from which all movements of the ladder could be controlled by electrically operated remote controls.

Tyne and Wear Fire Brigade continued to purchase the F series, while their neighbour Cleveland Fire Brigade had opted for the R series. The F131 was traditionally built and featured a Perkins 640 cubic-inch engine mated to the Allison four-speed automatic transmission. Conventional hinged lift-up locker doors were used throughout. A roof-mounted monitor on the offside of the appliance gave the ability to immediately direct a stream of water from an elevated position without the need to deploy any other equipment. The blue exhaust smoke is a characteristic of all Perkins V8 engines as they become older.

Chapter 8

1980–1990

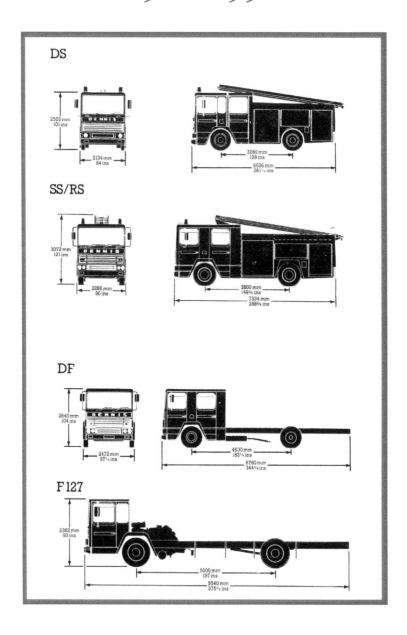

The 1990s saw the emergence of a new range of Dennis fire engines that were to become the most successful ever produced, with over 1,750 being manufactured. These were a continuation of the R series, but with an all-new steel cab. The RS (R Type Steel), which had a fixed cab, was introduced first, followed by the SS (Standard Specification), which had a tilting cab. The tilting cab gave easy access to the engine and chassis for maintenance purposes. Safety of the fire crew was improved by the steel cab and by the fitting of the Girling Skidcheck system – this was an anti-lock braking system and was the beginning of the introduction of electronic systems onto Dennis vehicles.

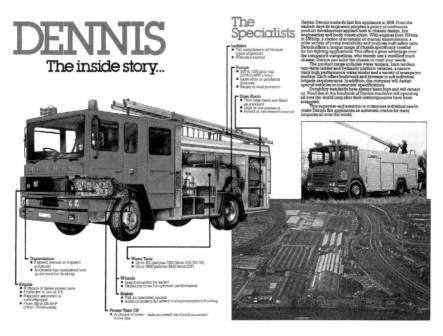

The Dennis DS was a successor to the D Type. With a narrow track of 7 feet compared to 7 feet 6 inches for the RS/SS and 8 feet for the DF, it was one of the narrowest fire engines available in the world. Combined with a short wheelbase, it was ideal for country fire stations. The Dennis DF was the heavyweight of the line up. As a gross vehicle weight of 17 tons was permitted, the chassis was used for foam/water tenders, hydraulic platforms and turntable ladder appliances.

A726 BTY is a DF133 with the Magirus DL30 ladder, while the appliance alongside is a standard SS with a unique body conversion. Originally supplied by Dennis as a pumping appliance, it was later converted by extending the chassis to accept the *Tinea* fire boat. Some brigades like London were still using Victorian fire stations where height was limited. Dennis therefore still provided the low-line Delta chassis in the form of the F127; on these they used the unproven French Camiva ladder. Although part of the Iveco Magirus group, the ladder had none of the reliability attributes of the Magirus equivalent and was unsatisfactory in service.

Despite trying to standardise on a rationalised product range, Dennis would still produce any style of fire appliance. Tyne and Wear Fire Brigade requested a control unit of huge proportions, resulting in this 40-foot-long machine. It was based on their Dennis Dominator double-deck bus chassis, with a rear-mounted Gardner 6ELX engine. Designed long before the technology for mobile telephones existed, side access panels enabled a direct connection to be made with the nearest telegraph pole to establish telephonic communication. A built-in silent generator provided a 240 V ring main, which also powered the roof-mounted air conditioning unit. Four control desks fitted with an array of VHF and UHF radio equipment allowed interoperability with neighbouring brigades as well as the fire ground.

Chapter 9

1990–2007

DENNIS moves into the 1990s with 'Rapier'

In introducing its newest vehicle, Dennis says that through its entirely new order of advanced chassis design it dramatically raises the standards of roadholding, manoeuvrability, acceleration and braking – the Rapier is the driver's machine, the firm says.

THE **STRENGTH** TO *DRIVE* ON

1991 saw the introduction of the Dennis Rapier. The design team was given the task of producing the world's most advanced fire-fighting appliance. The result was an appliance which more resembled the chassis of a racing car than that of a lorry. Even today over twenty years later, no other fire engine can match the performance of the Rapier. Universally loved by all who drove her, the Rapier set standards which may never be approached again. It was a tilt-cab design, but it was what lay beneath the cab that was so extraordinary!

The standard beam axle found on every other fire engine and large commercial vehicle had been replaced by independent front suspension. Each wheel could adapt to the road conditions, independently supported by coil springs which were hydraulically damped. The chassis was a backbone type produced from tubular stainless steel, which gave corrosion resistance. The front disk brakes were the same as those used to stop the huge Renault Magnum truck. Power came from a lightweight Cummins 6CTA six-cylinder turbocharged and aftercooled diesel engine producing 240 hp. Chassis/cab kerb weight was under 4½ tons. Inside the Rapier was a modern and spacious cab. Gear selection was by an electronic push-button selection box, which could cause problems as it was possible to select reverse accidently while travelling at full speed.

Later Rapiers had more rounded and attractive body styling to the cab. However, Dennis realised that not every chief fire officer was pleased to have their fire crew driving to incidents in a vehicle with the performance of a racing car and introduced a more conventional appliance, the Dennis Sabre. This had many attributes of the Rapier but was built on a conventional ladder-frame chassis. It became available in many variants including the XL (extra large), which could accommodate a crew of ten, and a HD (heavy duty) version, suitable for the mounting of turntable ladders.

More cab space for more crew and more equipment - the new Dennis XL firecab gives you extra scope to deliver more firepower, more cost effectively.

Comfortably accommodating up to ten fully equipped firefighters, the all stainless-steel Dennis XL firecab has been developed from the ECE crash-and-crush tested Dennis six-man firecab - ensuring the highest standards of crew safety and security.

With the Sabre well established, Dennis turned their design effort into making a lower-cost version which was called the Dagger. By opting for a less powerful engine and by removing some of the non-essential features of the Sabre, it was hoped that significant cost savings could be made. In practice this amounted to only £10,000, which resulted in little demand for the Dagger. The final variants of the Sabre were distinguished by small, round high-intensity discharge lamps. The last Sabre left the Guildford factory in 2007, just one year before they could celebrate a hundred years of fire engine production.

Acknowledgements

I would like to acknowledge Alexander-Dennis for permission to reproduce some of their fire engine promotional material and the Surrey History Service, who now hold all of the Dennis factory archive.

I am also grateful to fellow Dennis enthusiasts who have provided additional photographic material. These include: David Miller and Ric Carlyon of New Zealand, Frank Van Der Weeden, Ian Moore, Ron Henderson, Brett Clayton, Roger Mardon, Bob Wright, David McManus, Dennis Scott, Bob Lovelock, Mike Sowinski, Jonathon Gardiner, Paul Sturman, Nigel Bayes, Paul Stevens and Shane Casey.

Every attempt has been made to seek permission for copyright material used in this book. However, if we have inadvertently used copyright material without permission/ acknowledgement we apologise and will make the necessary correction at the first opportunity.